Abolitionists and Human Rights
Fighting for Emancipation

Leslie Beckett

NEW YORK

Published in 2017 by The Rosen Publishing Group, Inc.
29 East 21st Street, New York, NY 10010

Editor: Katie Kawa
Book Design: Samantha DeMartin

Photo Credits: Cover George Eastman House/Premium Archive/Getty Images; pp. 4, 11 (masthead) Hulton Archive/Getty Images; p. 5 Francis Miller/The LIFE Picture Collection/Getty Images; p. 7 Print Collector/Hulton Archive/Getty Images; p. 8 Lawrence Thornton/Archive Photos/Getty Images; pp. 9, 19 MPI/Archive Photos/ Getty Images; p. 10 https://commons.wikimedia.org/wiki/File:William-Lloyd-Garrison-by-Jocelyn,-1833.jpg; p. 11 (*Liberator* page) https://commons.wikimedia.org/wiki/File:1831_Liberator.jpg; p. 13 Stock Montage/ Archive Photos/Getty Images; p. 14 https://commons.wikimedia.org/wiki/File:Alanson_Fisher_-_Harriet_ Beecher_Stowe_-_Google_Art_Project.jpg; p. 15 https://commons.wikimedia.org/wiki/File:Edwin_Longsden_ Long_-_Uncle_Tom_and_Little_Eva.JPG; p. 16 (Sarah) https://commons.wikimedia.org/wiki/File:Sarah_Moore_ Grimke.jpg; p. 16 (Angelina) https://commons.wikimedia.org/wiki/File:Angelina_Emily_Grimke.jpg; p. 17 Universal History Archive/Universal Images Group/Getty Images; p. 20 https://commons.wikimedia.org/ wiki/File:Ole_Peter_Hansen_Balling_-_John_Brown_-_Google_Art_Project.jpg; p. 21 Everett Historical/ Shutterstock.com.

Library of Congress Cataloging-in-Publication Data

Names: Beckett, Leslie, author.
Title: Abolitionists and human rights : fighting for emancipation / Leslie
  Beckett.
Description: New York : PowerKids Press, 2016. | Series: Spotlight on
  American history | Includes index.
Identifiers: LCCN 2015047936 | ISBN 9781508149491 (pbk.) | ISBN 9781508149378 (library bound) | ISBN
9781508149163 (6 pack)
Subjects: LCSH: Abolitionists--Juvenile literature. | Antislavery
  movements--United States--Juvenile literature.
Classification: LCC E449 .B39 2016 | DDC 326/.8092--dc23
LC record available at http://lccn.loc.gov/2015047936

Manufactured in the United States of America

CPSIA Compliance Information: Batch #BS16PK: For further information contact Rosen Publishing, New York, New York at 1-800-237-9932.

CONTENTS

FREEDOM FIGHTERS

In the Declaration of Independence, it's written that "all men are created equal" and that they have the right to "Life, Liberty and the pursuit of Happiness." However, for nearly a century after those words were written, "all men" didn't really mean "all men." Millions of men, women, and children were taken from their homes in Africa and forced to work as slaves—first in the 13 British colonies, and then in the United States.

Slaves were treated as property and not as people. Abolitionists worked to change this way of thinking.

The abolitionist movement inspired many social justice movements that came after it, such as the civil rights movement.

Many people—especially plantation owners in the South—saw slavery as an important part of the American economy because of the cheap labor it provided. However, some men and women tried to abolish, or end, the **institution** of slavery. These people were known as abolitionists.

Abolitionists came from different backgrounds, but they were united in their goal of ending slavery. They paved the way for modern human rights **activists**.

THE EARLY ABOLITIONIST MOVEMENT

In 1619, the first slaves were brought to what would become the 13 British colonies. For the next century, very few people spoke out against the institution of slavery in North America. A movement called the **Enlightenment** led some people to question the morality of slavery. Also, some religious groups were known for their antislavery beliefs. Members of the Society of Friends, who were also known as Quakers, were some of the earliest abolitionists in the United States.

By the start of the 19th century, the abolitionist movement began to grow, especially in the North. By 1804, all U.S. states north of Maryland had agreed to abolish slavery. Four years later, a law was enacted that banned the **importation** of slaves to the United States.

Despite these victories for the cause of abolition, slaves in the South were still many years away from being freed. The southern economy depended on the cheap labor slaves provided, so many southerners were strongly opposed to abolition.

The economies of states in the North didn't depend on farming as much as the economies of southern states. As such, northern states didn't depend on slave labor in the same way southern states did. This made people in the North more open to abolitionist ideas.

A NEW AWAKENING

The abolitionist movement was deeply connected to religious beliefs. This became even truer after the Second Great Awakening. This was a religious **revival** that took place around the beginning of the 19th century. It led to the growth of certain Christian churches in the United States, such as the Methodist and Baptist churches.

The Great Methodist Camp Meeting, New York City, 1865

The Second Great Awakening also inspired a new period of social activism. During this time, more Americans began to take up the abolitionist cause. These Americans saw slavery as a sin against their fellow human beings. Before this period in American history, abolitionists often called for a

This image was used by abolitionist groups in Britain and the United States.

gradual end to slavery. However, as time passed, abolitionists began to call for immediate and total emancipation, or freedom, for slaves.

Groups began to form throughout the United States to push for immediate abolition. The most famous of these was the American Anti-Slavery Society, which was founded in 1833.

WILLIAM LLOYD GARRISON

One of the leaders of the American Anti-Slavery Society was William Lloyd Garrison, who was a newspaper editor and publisher as well as an outspoken abolitionist. When the American Anti-Slavery Society was founded in 1833, Garrison was chosen to write its Declaration of Sentiments, which stated the purpose and goals of the organization.

William Lloyd Garrison

Even before Garrison helped lead the American Anti-Slavery Society, he proudly made his abolitionist views public knowledge. On January 1, 1831, he published the first issue of his abolitionist newspaper, the *Liberator*. In his writings for the paper, he called for the immediate abolition of slavery,

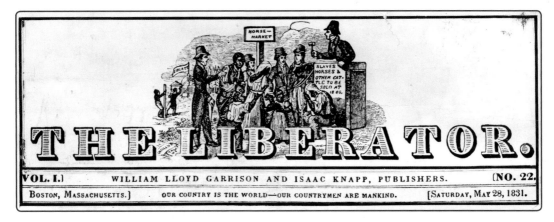

Garrison published his last issue of the Liberator *in 1865, after seeing his abolitionist dreams become a reality.*

which was still considered a **radical** idea at the time.

Garrison's radical beliefs were sometimes a problem with his fellow abolitionists. He believed in allowing women to participate in the American Anti-Slavery Society. He also believed the U.S. Constitution supported slavery, which led to his antigovernment views. Many abolitionists didn't agree with these beliefs.

FREDERICK DOUGLASS SPEAKS OUT

Despite Garrison's radical beliefs, his passion for the abolitionist cause inspired many people to speak out against slavery. One of those people was Frederick Douglass. Douglass was a former slave who escaped to freedom in the North. He was inspired by Garrison's writings and speeches to become an outspoken abolitionist, even though that was unsafe for a former slave.

Douglass was known for his public speaking ability as well as his writing. In 1845, he published his autobiography, or the story of his life. *Narrative of the Life of Frederick Douglass, an American Slave, Written By Himself* opened many people's eyes to what a slave's life was really like. In 1847, Douglass began publishing his own antislavery newspaper, which was called the *North Star.*

Douglass and Garrison eventually had a falling out over their different views. For example, while Garrison saw the U.S. Constitution as a proslavery document, Douglass believed it could be used to support the abolitionist cause.

Douglass gave his first antislavery speech in Nantucket, Massachusetts, in 1841. From that moment on, he continued to speak out about his life as a slave and the importance of fighting for the abolition of slavery.

THE POWER OF THE PEN

Both Garrison and Douglass knew the written word was one of the most powerful weapons they could use to fight for the abolition of slavery. Abolitionist newspapers, such as the *Liberator* and the *North Star*, helped spread the word to many about their cause. Books also became an important way of making large numbers of people aware of the horrors of slavery.

Douglass's autobiography was one of many slave narratives published in the mid-1800s. A slave narrative is an account of slavery written by someone who'd been a slave. Other famous slave narratives included

Harriet Beecher Stowe

Shown here is a painting of a scene from Uncle Tom's Cabin.

Solomon Northup's *Twelve Years a Slave* and Harriet Jacobs's *Incidents in the Life of a Slave Girl, Written by Herself.*

Fictional accounts of slavery also moved many to join the abolitionist cause. Harriet Beecher Stowe published *Uncle Tom's Cabin* as a novel in 1852. This novel, which told the story of a slave named Uncle Tom, helped create support for the abolitionist movement.

EQUAL RIGHTS FOR ALL

The abolitionist movement had close ties to the women's rights movement. Many women supported the abolitionist cause, and some leading abolitionists were also active supporters of granting American women more rights.

Sarah and Angelina Grimké were sisters from South Carolina who became outspoken abolitionists.

Sarah Grimké

Angelina Grimké

Susan B. Anthony and Elizabeth Cady Stanton

While some of their fellow abolitionists, such as William Lloyd Garrison, supported their statements against slavery, others wanted them to stay silent because they were women.

Frederick Douglass was known not only as an antislavery activist but also as a women's rights activist. He believed that all people—regardless of race or gender—deserved equal rights. He even attended the First Women's Rights Convention in Seneca Falls, New York, in 1848. Douglass worked alongside famous women's rights leaders Elizabeth Cady Stanton and Susan B. Anthony as part of the American Equal Rights Association. This organization worked from 1866 to 1869 to fight for equal rights for all Americans.

A POLITICAL ISSUE

Abolishing slavery wasn't just a social issue; it was also a political issue. While William Lloyd Garrison and his followers opposed any kind of political approach to abolishing slavery, other abolitionists were active in politics.

In 1840, abolitionists who sided against Garrison formed the Liberty Party. This political party was known for its antislavery beliefs. In the presidential elections of 1840 and 1844, abolitionist James G. Birney was the Liberty Party's candidate. In 1848, many members of the Liberty Party joined the Free-Soil Party. This political party's goals included outlawing the spread of slavery, especially into the new territories the United States had acquired from Mexico in the U.S.-Mexican War. The Free-Soil Party's **slogan** was "free soil, free speech, free labor, and free men."

By the mid-1850s, these smaller parties had **disbanded**, and most politically active abolitionists became members of the Republican Party. This party eventually supported the idea of the complete abolition of slavery.

Shown here is an image created in support of the Free-Soil Party in 1848. Former president Martin Van Buren ran as the Free-Soil Party candidate in that year's presidential election. Charles Francis Adams was the party's vice presidential candidate.

JOHN BROWN'S RAID

While most abolitionists took a nonviolent approach to ending slavery, some believed the only way to end the institution for good was by force. John Brown was one of these abolitionists. He planned to take control of a

federal **armory** in Harpers Ferry, which was part of Virginia at the time but is part of West Virginia now. Brown believed he could use the weapons in the armory to start a slave revolt and attack slaveholders.

John Brown

While Brown didn't start the revolt he'd hoped for, his actions did help push the country toward a war that would lead to the end of slavery.

On October 16, 1859, Brown led a group of 21 men to Harpers Ferry. Although Brown and his men took over the armory at first, they couldn't get any slaves to join their fight. Eventually, they were surrounded and forced to surrender.

Brown was **executed** on December 2, 1859. His actions helped drive the North and South further apart on the issues of slavery and abolition. Brown's **raid** was a major event on the path to the American Civil War.

THE END OF SLAVERY

The North and the South had very different views of slavery, abolition, and many other issues. These differences eventually led to war. The American Civil War was fought from 1861 to 1865 between the North, which was also known as the Union, and the South, which became known as the Confederate States of America or the Confederacy.

Although the abolition of slavery wasn't a goal of the Union at first, it became an important aspect of the war following President Abraham Lincoln's Emancipation Proclamation, which was delivered in 1863. This proclamation said the slaves in the Confederacy were free. However, the true end of the institution of slavery occurred with the ratification, or official approval, of the 13th **Amendment** to the U.S. Constitution in 1865, following the Union's victory in the war. While the fight for total equality was still far from over, slavery was officially abolished in the United States.

GLOSSARY

activist (AK-tuh-vihst): A person who takes action in support of or against an issue.

amendment (uh-MEHND-muhnt): A change in the words or meaning of a law or document, such as a constitution.

armory (AR-muh-ree): A place where weapons are kept.

disband (dihs-BAND): To end an organization or group.

Enlightenment (in-LY-tuhn-muhnt): A movement in the 18th century marked by the rejection of traditional beliefs in favor of logic and science.

execute (EK-suh-kyoot): To kill someone as punishment for a crime.

importation (ihm-por-TAY-shuhn): The act of bringing a product into a country to be sold.

institution (ihn-stuh-TOO-shuhn): A custom, practice, or law that is accepted and used by many people.

radical (RAA-duh-kuhl): Extreme and not shared by most people.

raid (RAYD): A surprise attack on an enemy.

revival (rih-VY-vuhl): A period of renewed religious interest.

slogan (SLOH-guhn): A phrase used to express a position or a goal.

INDEX

PRIMARY SOURCE LIST

Page 10: Portrait of William Lloyd Garrison. Created by Nathaniel Jocelyn. 1833. Oil on wood. Now kept at the National Portrait Gallery, Smithsonian Institution, Washington, D.C.

Page 11: Front page of the first issue of the *Liberator*. Created by William Lloyd Garrison. 1831. Paper. Now kept at the Library Company of Philadelphia, Philadelphia, Pennsylvania.

Page 14: Portrait of Harriet Beecher Stowe. Created by Alanson Fisher. 1853. Oil on canvas. Now kept at the National Portrait Gallery, Smithsonian Institution, Washington, D.C.

Page 19: *Grand Democratic Free Soil Banner*. Copy of original lithograph and watercolor print by Nathaniel Currier. Original now kept at the Library of Congress, Prints and Photographs Division, Washington, D.C.

WEBSITES

Due to the changing nature of Internet links, PowerKids Press has developed an online list of websites related to the subject of this book. This site is updated regularly. Please use this link to access the list: www.powerkidslinks.com/soah/abol